Let Us Be Grateful

Sri Mata Amritanandamayi Devi

Let Us Be Grateful

Sri Mata Amritanandamayi Devi

Compiled by Swami Jnanamritananda Puri
Translated by Rajani Menon

Published by:
Mata Amritanandamayi Center
P.O. Box 613
San Ramon, CA 94583
United States

In India:
www.amritapuri.org
inform@amritapuri.org

In USA:
amma.org

In Europe:
www.amma-europe.org

Let Us Be Grateful

Sri Mata Amritanandamayi Devi

Mata Amritanandamayi Center
San Ramon, California, USA

Introduction

There is a beautiful mantra in the *Atharva Vēda* that highlights the inseparable bond between us and Mother Earth:

> *mātā bhūmiḥ putrōham pṛthivyāḥ*
> The earth is my mother, and I am the child of the earth. (2.12.1.12)

As children of Mother Earth, it is our *dharma* (duty) to love and serve her. The ethos of protecting the earth and preserving her resources informs the culture founded on Sanātana Dharma.[1] The mother who gave birth to us carried us in her womb for nine months. Mother Earth protects and nurtures us in her womb for all time. But are we doing our dharma as her children? When the child in the womb hurts the mother, it causes hardship for itself, as it is a part of the mother. By the same token,

[1] Literally 'Eternal Religion' or 'Eternal Way of Life,' the original and traditional name of Hinduism.

the troubles we are facing now are a consequence of our ill-treatment of nature.

Yet Mother Nature, the very embodiment of love, patiently forgives all our mistakes and protects us. But do we ever think about her? Are we following in the footsteps of our ancestors, who protected nature? At least now, let us be ready to right our wrongs. This compilation of talks by Amma reminds us of the need to be grateful to Mother Nature, and provides practical guidance on how we can care for her.

Publisher

"

Nature is Kāmadhēnu — the divine, wish-fulfilling cow that bestows prosperity on all. But at present, it is like an ailing cow whose udders have dried up and which is on the verge of death. The number of forests on earth has dwindled. Food is becoming scarce. Pure air and water are no longer available. There is an increase in the incidence of diseases. If we take from nature only enough to sustain ourselves, there will be sufficient food, water and clothes for everyone. Nature will regain her vitality and once again become like Kāmadhēnu.

Amma

LET US BE GRATEFUL for nature's bounty. The mother who gave birth to us may keep us in her lap for our first two or three years, at most. But Mother Earth bears our weight our whole life. Our body came from this earth, and even while spitting and stamping on her, she continues to bless us lovingly. We sustain ourselves on the abundant produce that the earth provides. Even the breast milk we drank as infants came from Mother Earth, for the food that nourished our mothers was provided by Mother Earth. It was this sustenance that enabled her to nurture us with breast milk. So, we are even more indebted to Mother Earth than to the mother who gave birth to us. That being the case, shouldn't we remain ever grateful to her?

Sanātana Dharma worships the sun, moon, trees, plants, birds, animals, earth and everything in it, seeing them all as God. In truth, the worship is nothing but an expression of profound gratitude for the good they do to humankind.

Every morning, many people gaze at the sun, prostrate to it and pray. They chant the *Āditya Hṛdaya.*[2] Some ask, "Isn't this practice primitive? Why pray to the sun?" and other such questions.

Are we mindful of the fact that life exists on this planet only because of the sun? It is from sunlight that we receive Vitamin D, which is essential for strong bones and muscles. Doctors advise us to spend some time in the sun daily for our health. Sunshine is needed to stimulate the brain, to form memories and to retain information. Many countries that lack sunlight report a higher incidence of depression. The number of suicides is also greater in these places.

Diseases flourish when the sun's heat decreases and cold weather sets in. In Kerala, it rains heavily in the month of *Karkkiṭaka,*[3] when dark clouds cover the sun and there is less sunshine. At this time, there is an outbreak of gastrointestinal diseases

[2] 'Heart of the Sun-god,' a hymn glorifying the sun.
[3] The last month in the Malayāḷam calendar, coinciding approximately with the period from July – August. Typically, it marks the peak of the monsoon.

and epidemics. This shows how vital the sun's presence is to life.

The sun gains nothing by our worship. It is we who benefit from the sun. So, what is wrong with seeing the sun as a manifestation of God, who nourishes and protects us? Is there any place where God is not? If someone picks up an object that has fallen from our hands and gives it back to us, we thank him or her. If we do not express our gratitude in one way or another, doesn't it show a lack of gratitude and inner refinement? Why do we forget this?

Even the tiniest bud in a dense forest blossoms only because of sunlight. There would be no life on earth without sunlight and heat. A grateful heart will regard the sun with reverence.

In earlier days, the *tulasī* (holy basil) used to be grown in front of every Hindu home. After their morning bath, the family members would water the plant, circumambulate it reverentially, and sip a few drops of water in which the tulasī leaves had been immersed.

The tulasī is a medicinal plant. If someone had a cold, the elders in the family would advise him or her to boil water with tulasī leaves and to drink it. The tulasī is a natural immune booster and an antidote to many illnesses. Why should we question the practice of circumambulating the tulasī? This expression of reverence is an expression of thanksgiving, not just to the tulasī but to all fruits and vegetables, which are equally food and medicine.

The Hindu tradition also honors the sacred *bilva* (Aegle marmelos or stone apple) tree. Its leaves and fruit also have great medicinal value. The holy water given in temples as *prasād* (consecrated offering) is often infused with tulasī and bilva leaves. Drinking a few drops of this holy water daily will enhance our immunity.

Our ancestors used to draw *kōlams*—a floor design made with rice flour—every morning; even now, there are people who do this. It is not merely a decoration; it is also *bhūta yajña*, a ritual offering of food to creatures; ants and other tiny insects eat rice flour. In this way, we can prevent them from entering our kitchens and storerooms in search of food. As these creatures play a significant role in keeping our surroundings clean, we can consider the practice of drawing a *kōlam* a gesture of gratitude to them.

In fact, every traditional observance in Sanātana Dharma is as an act of giving thanks for the help rendered by different beings in nature. All of nature gives us immeasurably more than what we offer. Therefore, we ought to view these rituals as acts of loving and serving all beings.

Nothing Can Atone for Ingratitude

We can redress our wrongs by doing good deeds. But nothing can atone for ingratitude. If we do not show our gratitude to nature for all the good she does, we will face a backlash. We must be grateful for all that we get, whether small or big. The expressions of gratitude our ancestors felt for nature's munificence evolved into rituals of worship. There is a goal behind each traditional ritual. No observance is meaningless. Each ritual is based on an understanding of human psychology. In the long run, those who observe the rituals are the ones who will benefit the most.

Many *śānti mantras* (peace prayers) were regularly chanted in Gurukulas[4] throughout Bhārat (India). This mantra is one among them:

---

[4] The *kula* (clan) of the Guru, a Gurukula is a traditional school where students would stay with the Guru for the

ōm sarvē bhavantu sukhinaḥ
sarvē santu nirāmayāḥ
sarvē bhadrāṇi paśyantu
mā kaścid duḥkha-bhāg bhavēt
ōm śāntiḥ śāntiḥ śāntiḥ

> May everyone be at peace. May no one be ill. May everyone see only the auspicious. May no one grieve. Peace, peace, peace![5]

Our ancestors did not pray, "May I alone benefit," or "May we alone flourish." Their concern was not for the well-being of humankind alone. On the contrary, they prayed for the happiness of all living beings. They knew that happiness for human beings alone was not possible, as our well-being is linked to that of all other beings. We can survive only if there is harmony in nature.

Bow Down in Reverence

In Sanātana Dharma, the Creator and creation are not separate. Divine consciousness permeates

---

entire duration of their scriptural studies.

[5] 'Peace' is thrice repeated to indicate respite from three types of suffering: *ādhyātmika* (bodily suffering and mental anguish), *ādhibhautika* (suffering caused by others) and *ādhidaivika* (suffering caused by time, nature and fate).

everything. We worship animals, birds, the sun, mountains and rivers. In doing so, we are worshipping the one God that dwells in all of them. There is nothing other than God in the universe; nothing is separate from Him. Those who do not grasp the practical benefits of such worship disparagingly label it primitive.

Amma would like to share her experience. She was born and grew up in the Alappad village, which is located between the ocean and the backwaters. People used to bathe in the backwaters when its waters were cleaner. Amma also used to do that when she was a child. Damayanti-amma (Amma's mother) would say, "Don't urinate in the water. The river is Dēvī (Goddess)." Even though Amma would feel the urge to urinate when wading into the cold water, Damayanti-amma's words would come to mind. And like a switch being turned off, Amma would be able to curb the urge. It is not the river that benefits from this, but those who bathe or swim there. If the water we bathe or swim in is polluted, we will be susceptible to disease. That is why no one is allowed to wear dirty clothes in a swimming pool; doing so will contaminate the water. Those who enter the pool might fall sick. In fact, ear infections are one of the most common water-borne diseases.

Our ancestors advised us to see water bodies as divine and to keep them pristine for our own benefit. It is also said that creation arose from water. Can we survive without water? Without water, how can we cultivate the food we eat? Ancient civilizations all over the world were situated on riverbanks. We worship rivers to show appreciation for the blessings they bestow on us.

Some people mock us, saying, "You worship trees, don't you?" Indeed, it is true that trees are worshiped in Sanātana Dharma. If we reflect on all that trees do for us, we will bow down our heads in reverence before them.

In Ernakulam, waste used to be dumped on an island not far from AIMS Hospital.[6] Even though the island was thoroughly cleaned as part of the Amala Bharatam campaign,[7] tests revealed that the soil there was highly toxic. We then planted

---

[6] Amrita Institute of Medical Sciences.

[7] A campaign that Amma launched in 2010 to clean India's public places and national highways.

rāmaccam (vetiver) and other types of trees on the island. After three years, we tested the soil once again. This time, there was no trace of poison. Scientific journals have published papers attesting to how the roots of the rāmaccam and other trees purify contaminated soil. Trees and plants succeed where technology and human effort fail. So, one of the reasons we worship plants and trees is that they purify the earth.

Like trees, many other creatures also help to purify the air. The whale plays a significant role. We know that trees absorb carbon dioxide and release oxygen into the atmosphere, thus purifying it. A single whale produces as much oxygen as is produced by a large number of trees. Not only that, great whales accumulate tons of carbon dioxide in their bodies and carry it down to the seafloor when they die. Shouldn't we venerate whales? Scientists are now aware of the vital role that marine microorganisms play in releasing oxygen into the atmosphere. If oxygen becomes depleted in the atmosphere, the earth will become uninhabitable.

There was a very deep well in Kollam. Four men went down the well to clean it and died because they inhaled poisonous air. There was no oxygen in the depths of the well. We are able to breathe fresh air and live on earth because of a diverse array of life forms. But do we bother to think about them even once in our lifetime? Won't it be a pity if we do not express our heartfelt gratitude to them? Can we not at least offer our prostrations to them mentally?

Alas, owing to our greed, many types of flora and fauna are becoming extinct. We use pesticides to protect our crops from pests that feed on the crops only to satiate their hunger. However, we encroach upon and destroy nature because of our greed. Hence, aren't human beings the most dangerous pests on earth?

Sometimes, we insult someone by saying, "You're just like a dog!" But a dog has abilities we lack. For example, it has an acute sense of smell. This is why dogs are used by the police to sniff out drugs and criminals. Likewise, God has blessed each species with unique abilities. Therefore, we ought to revere every being in creation.

Sanātana Dharma also has great reverence for mountains. They force air to rise and hence cool. The cooling makes water vapor condense and fall as rain. The tiny rivulets of water that flow down the mountains gradually become rivers. Many varieties of medicinal plants grow on mountain slopes. Mountains thus serve humanity in so many ways. By worshiping them, we are giving thanks for their generous assistance.

In earlier days, bulls were used to plow fields. People relied on bulls and bullock carts for business and transport. Human beings drink cow's milk and consume various dairy products. Milk from an indigenous cow is the ideal substitute for breast milk. Many people live on the earnings from a single cow. We feed them hay, rice husk and rice water. What they give in return is of far greater value. Knowing this, we revere the cow as a mother—Gō-mātā. Kāmadhēnu, Kalpavṛkṣa, Nandi and Garuḍa are all divine symbols of our reverence for all creatures in creation.[8]

[8] Kāmadhēnu is a mythical wish-fulfilling cow. Kalpavṛkṣa is a mythical wish-fulfilling tree. Nandi, the bull, is the vehicle of Lord Śiva. Garuḍa, the eagle, is Lord Viṣṇu's vehicle.

Nothing is Insignificant in Nature

There is nothing insignificant in nature. If the engine of a plane malfunctions, it cannot take off. One missing screw can compromise the safety of a flight. Likewise, nothing in nature is insignificant. We should not despise or disparage something just because it is tiny.

The first thing we ought to do upon waking up is to bend down and reverentially touch Bhūmīdēvī, Goddess Earth. It is we who will benefit from this action. Bending down is a simple exercise that stretches the body after sleeping for hours. It also regulates blood flow. When we start our day with the awareness that nature, which protects and loves us, is our mother, all the forces of nature become favorable to us. God needs nothing from us. The sun does not need candlelight to illuminate its path.

Ayurvedic medicines are prepared with a mix of herbs. For instance, the oil that many people in India rub on their bodies before bathing is prepared with an array of ingredients — *candan* (sandal), *raktacandan* (red sandalwood), *veḷḷakoṭṭam* (Indian costus), *devatāram* (cedar), *añjana-kallu* (surma stone), *pacca-karpūram* (natural camphor) and *kayyōnni nīru* (juice of the *bhriṅgarāj* flower), for example—and not just one component. Likewise, nature is not restricted to just one species but includes birds, animals, insects, aquatic creatures and human beings. It is the law of nature for one animal to become food for another. This is nature's way of ensuring that no species proliferates disproportionately. This law does not disturb the harmony in nature. It is because of other lifeforms, both plant and animal, that we can breathe in pure air, drink pure water, and get food to eat. In fact, we exist only because of their grace.

However, no species other than human beings destroy nature. We take great pride in our intellect, and yet we pollute the air, adulterate food, level mountains, and contaminate rivers. We release toxic chemicals into the rivers, thus killing many forms of aquatic life. We have hunted many birds, animals and fish to extinction, and razed many a forest. We are solely responsible for the current plight of nature. Yet, in spite of the atrocities we have inflicted on nature, she still offers us a conducive place to live. We ought to be grateful to her.

Don't Saw Off the Branch on Which You Sit

Scientists invented chemical fertilizers and pesticides to combat severe food shortages and to increase harvests. They also provided specific instructions on the correct dosage, as overdosing adversely affects health and longevity and might even cause death. But many farmers, interested only in increasing their yield to maximize profits, disregard these instructions and use chemical fertilizers and pesticides indiscriminately.

While their indiscriminate use might be profitable in the short run, it will eventually bring about the destruction of both nature and humankind. It is comparable to cutting down the branch on which we are sitting. If we try to paint a grimy wall, the paint will not stick to the wall. Similarly, the earth will eventually stop responding to fertilizers, as many microorganisms that enhance the vitality of the soil have been killed as a consequence of adding excessive chemical fertilizers to the soil. Already, the soil in many parts of the world has become unsuitable for cultivation. Furthermore, with the prices of chemical fertilizers and pesticides escalating, farming is becoming unprofitable to many.

Many farmers commit suicide because of the distress caused by a low crop yield and high expenses.

Poisonous fumes emitted by factories have polluted the air; the toxic chemicals released into the water have contaminated it; and the waste dumped has poisoned the earth. Our unchecked greed has wreaked havoc on nature.

Amma is not against expansion and modernization. We can have what we want, but we should take only what we need. We must give up our selfish concern for only our needs and those of our family. Future generations also have a right to this land. We must realize that in polluting the earth, we are paving the way for the destruction of the human race.

In the past, if there was a cut or wound on our hand, cow dung would be applied to it, and it would heal fast, whereas today, applying cow dung will cause the wound to become septic. This is because cows used to be fed with the husk of grains grown without chemical fertilizers, and so, the husk was free from all contaminants. The cows would also be fed with cakes of sesame, coconut and peanuts after the oil had been extracted from them. The hay they fed on was also free of chemicals. In those days, cows could graze on wide pastures of grass, small plants and shrubs. The dung, urine and milk of these cows were medicinal. *Pañcagavya,*[9] prepared with these ingredients, was medicinal. But now, cows are given artificial cattle feed and dried rice stalks to which excessive chemical fertilizers and pesticides had been added. How then can a cow's milk, dung and urine be medicinal?

These days, it is rare to find someone who does not own a vehicle. There are families of four in which all four members have their own vehicles. No one thinks about the pollution caused by smoke from so many vehicles. And if they are aware of it, they do not think that environmental conservation and protection is their responsibility.

Instead of traveling alone, we can save fuel by giving others a ride. With fewer vehicles, pollution will also be reduced. If there are 4,000 or 5,000 people living in a neighborhood, one person can drive three or four others working for the same company, and share the fuel bill among themselves. They can

[9] Mixture made from five ingredients: cow dung, urine, milk, yoghurt and ghee.

also take turns offering each other rides. This will reduce traffic and travel time. Road accidents will decrease. We can make new friends. We need not offer rides to strangers, only to people we know and trust. Through such agreements, we can help to sustain the harmony in nature.

The Foresight of our Forebears

Modern scientific inquiry has validated the science behind the words of our forebears. They advised against gazing directly at the sun during eclipses. Instead, they would fill a large vessel with water, mix a little cow dung into it, and look at the reflection of the sun in the water. Today, scientists warn us that looking directly at a solar eclipse will harm the eyes. They advise us to wear dark glasses if we wish to do so. Our ancestors already showed us how to view a solar eclipse, without causing harm to the eyes or spending unnecessary money. Our ancestors have indeed bequeathed to us many pearls of wisdom.

The *Bhāgavata Purāṇa,*[10] a text of antiquity, declares, "Forests will make way for houses; houses

---

[10] One of the 18 Purāṇas known also as *Śrīmad Bhāgavatam*, it is a Sanskrit text that narrates the life, pastimes and

will become shops; people will stop going to temples and consume intoxicants; the son will eat the father; and the father will eat the son." These predictions are coming true literally. We have encroached upon and cleared 70% of forests and built homes there. Many homes are like shops now, with the number of people engaged in doing online business at home increasing by the day.

Long ago, when people felt sad, they called out to God. But now they turn to alcohol and other intoxicants. What is happening today in places of worship in the name of festivals? The music, dance and drama performed there awaken base emotions. Sometimes, they culminate in verbal abuse and physical fights, confirming the prophesy that "people will stop going to temples and consume intoxicants." Instead of competing and fighting in the name of worship, we must try to assimilate spiritual principles. Then we will become patient, loving and compassionate to others. There have been reports of drug addicts attacking their own mothers or their own children. Once addicted to

---

teachings of the various incarnations of Lord Viṣṇu (the Sustainer in the Hindu Trinity), chiefly that of Lord Kṛṣṇa.

drugs, people will disregard familial bonds and will not hesitate to attack or kill each other. Relationships have come to such a sorry state.

It was written in the Purāṇas[11] that in the *Kali-yuga,*[12] one will not be able to distinguish men and women by their external appearance or clothing. This has come true. Girls have short hair and walk around in jeans and shirts. Boys now grow long hair.

Amma is not trying to restrict anyone's freedom. She is just pointing out that many ancient prophecies have come true. The weather is no longer predictable. Heatwaves come and stay for extended periods. Rains pour relentlessly. Torrential downpours can trigger landslides and mudflows that cause massive destruction.

---

[11] Compendium of stories, including the biographies and stories of gods, saints, kings and great people; allegories and chronicles of great historical events that aim to make the teachings of the Vēdas simple and available to all.

[12] According to the Hindu worldview, the universe passes through a cycle of four *yugas* (epochs). Dharma declines from age to age. The fourth and present epoch is known as the Kali-yuga.

It is said that in the Kali-yuga, there will not be even a spark of compassion; even cows will stop giving milk. These words are becoming a reality.

Learn to Give

Today, we have become more selfish and less generous, interested more in taking than in giving. Even while making a cup of tea, we think, "Do I really need to add so much milk, sugar or tea?" With a view only to increasing our profits, we think of ways in which we can reduce the quantity of whatever we are giving. Through such selfishness, we are ruining ourselves.

The devotion of our ancestors was neither blind nor primitive. They taught that it is more important to change our *manaḥsthiti* (attitudes) than the *paristhiti* (external environment). If we can adapt to changing circumstances, we will be happy anywhere. But if we lack this training, we will have sleepless nights even in air-conditioned rooms. Our ancestors gave equal importance to gaining an education for how to live and gaining an education to make a living. Today, the scope of education has become confined to acquiring occupational skills.

When education is centered around acquiring knowledge of the external world, we can gain the skills needed to earn money. But money in itself does not confer peace or contentment; only a calm mind does. Spiritual education teaches us how to gain serenity of mind and to live with the right values. Spirituality teaches us to let go of the notions of 'I' and 'mine,' and to love and serve humankind and other beings in creation. The *ṛṣis* (ancient seers) worshiped all of nature, not from fear but love. They regarded nature with gratitude because all creatures, from the tiny honeybee to the great whale, create a conducive environment for us to live in. In return, we must show our gratitude through an attitude of reverence to nature and by protecting her.

Traditionally in Kerala, farming would start on *Pattām-udayam*, the tenth sunrise after *Viṣu.*[13] On that day, saplings would be planted in each home. Damayanti-amma used to prepare saplings for planting on Pattām-udayam. The sun is considered most potent on that day. We can stave off

[13] Popular Hindu festival celebrated in Kerala and which coincides with the spring equinox.

starvation only if there is a good yield. For that, sunlight is vital. Farmers were aware of this, and Pattām-udayam was a festive celebration for them.

There are other festivals related to farming. *Pongal*[14] is one among them. In earlier days, farmers depended mainly on cattle for their agricultural activities. *Māṭṭu-pongal* pays homage to the service that cattle render. During *Makara-pongal*, we gratefully remember the sun-god, who protects the whole world, and offer him *Pongāla-naivēdya*—a traditional pudding made of harvest rice boiled in milk and jaggery. We must be ever thankful to all those who help us, whether they are humans, animals, birds, planets or stars. The same divine consciousness shines in all.

Pitṛ-tarpaṇa—Offering to Ancestors

Many say that it is superstitious to perform rituals aimed at satisfying and pleasing dead ancestors; instead, we should protect and take care of our elders while they are alive. True, we should see to it that our parents lack nothing and lovingly take care of them when they are alive. But do all

[14] Three-day harvest festival, which include Māṭṭu-pongal and Sūrya-pongal.

that they did to help us and all the hardship they endured to raise us cease to matter once they die? What is wrong with paying respects to them at least once a year after they have died? Those who do not believe in rituals for the dead can regard the rituals as expressions of gratitude.

There are layers of meaning to each ritual formulated by our ancestors. Those who criticize them do not make an effort to understand the rituals. How can a limited human being understand the secrets of the universe? To know them, we must have insight. To gain insight and perceive the truth, we need to live an ascetic life; our scriptures are nothing but the utterances of ascetics.

Many ask what the point is of performing the *Bali*[15] ritual. The main reason is to give thanks to our ancestors for the body, wealth and culture they gifted us. The offering of rice becomes food for crows and fish, and thus helps to sustain other creatures. Suppose we send an e-mail to someone living in a remote corner of the world. Won't it

[15] Also known as *Vāvu-bali*, it is a sacred ritual performed on no-moon days in the month of *Karkkiṭaka* (July – August) to propitiate the departed souls of ancestors.

reach them if the address is correct? Similarly, when we think of the one who has died and make a single-minded resolve to help them, our gesture will definitely benefit that *jīva* (soul). Death is not the ultimate destruction. It destroys only the body, which is made of the five elements. After death, the jīva accepts another body based on the *puṇya* (merits) and *pāpa* (demerits) gained through the deeds of its past life.

Many occurrences prove the existence of the individual soul even after the death of the body. Suppose we see an airplane take off and disappear into the clouds. If someone tells us that there is no plane in the sky, we know without doubt that it is up there. Not being able to see now what we had clearly seen earlier does not mean it no longer exists. Likewise, even when the body ceases to exist after death, the jīva remains.

As part of the Bali ritual, people perform *annadānam*, another sacred tradition of offering food to the poor as an act of gratitude to their ancestors. Does not society benefit by this? Why ignore these benefits? There are many facets to each of the traditions and rituals of Sanātana Dharma. Instead of remaining blind to their practical benefits, we must strive to understand them by approaching Sanātana Dharma with respect.

Ponds and Sacred Groves

Many people consider the worship of trees and practices like circumambulating them foolish. In earlier days, many homes had ponds and sacred groves. People worshiped the groves, considering them the realm of divine beings. Our forebears held sacred groves in great reverence and entered them in a spirit of worship. These groves were homes to a great number and variety of trees that purified the atmosphere. An oil lamp would be lit in the *sarppakkāvu*, a grove believed to be inhabited by snakes. An offering of *nūṙum pālum* — turmeric added to tender coconut water and milk — would be kept for the serpents. This was not superstition but an act of gratitude to snakes, who control the rat population, which would otherwise destroy crops and eat the grains in storage. Members of the *Puḷḷuvar* community would sing songs of worship dedicated to serpent deities in sarppakkāvus. The belief is that the snakes enjoy this music. As for *nūṙum pālum*, people have seen snakes bathing in the offering.

Today, there are sanctuaries that protect and ensure the survival of animals, birds and other creatures facing extinction. The sacred groves were sanctuaries to a wide variety of birds and other creatures in a harmonious ecosystem, a realm of biodiversity. Our predecessors did not pluck a single leaf unnecessarily from the trees in the sacred grove; they did not harm any creature either. In fact, they protected the diverse plant and animal species. Through their customs and way of life, our ancestors made coming generations aware that human beings are a part of nature.

Most of the trees in sacred groves have medicinal properties. The breeze that comes into contact with the leaves and branches purifies the atmosphere, thus benefiting those who breathe in the air here. Rainwater from the surroundings would flow into and fill the ponds in the grove; the water would not flow elsewhere. Nowadays, we dig rain-pits to prevent water from flowing away. In those days, ponds were the catchment basins. Taking a dip in a pond near a sacred grove is unlike taking a shower in a bathroom. The ponds were surrounded by plants and trees of medicinal value, and their healing properties would infuse the atmosphere and the water.

It was also believed that some sacred groves were imbued with the presence of the *paradēvata*—the family deity worshiped over centuries by the ancestors. There is also the custom of worshiping ancestors known as Yōgīśvara. After fulfilling their family responsibilities, some ancestors devoted their lives to intense and disciplined penance until they departed from this world. Such ascetics were called Yōgīśvara.

People living in the locality believed that the sacred groves, ponds and the divine beings present in the groves would protect them. They considered the ritual offerings and worship that were conducted there to be expressions of their gratitude. There were ponds adjoining temples also, and devotees would bathe here before entering the temple to pray. Science now recognizes the crucial role that ponds, wells and vast acres of fields play in water conservation.

As humans became more selfish, they filled up ponds and destroyed sacred groves. They also razed forests, which are home to wild animals. As a result, these animals have trespassed places of human habitation and are destroying crops on a large scale. Rats and other pests have proliferated, leading to the destruction of crops. To deal with them, farmers resort to pesticides. Scientists are genetically modifying plants. Research must be done on the effects of such modifications on our health. Modern feeds for chickens consist of formulations and include medications fortified by chemical supplements. Artificial ecosystems have been created to increase the number of eggs laid substantially. The nutritional value of such eggs is much less than those laid by free-range hens living in a natural environment. Similar methods have been adopted to increase the yield of milk in cows. Ducks are taken to forage in rice fields that have been sprayed with toxic pesticides. Traces of poison have been found in eggs laid by ducks that forage in these fields. We are interested only in maximizing profits. For the sake of financial gain, we are ready to compromise the health of another.

In earlier days, not many canoes plied the backwaters. The canoes did not have outboard motors either. Nowadays, there are hundreds of canoes and boats in the backwaters, many of them with diesel engines. As a result, the flesh of fish and crabs from the backwaters tastes and smells of diesel. The pollution and contamination on land and sea are pushing many creatures to the brink of extinction. Can humankind exist on this earth without other living creatures?

The environmental problems caused by the rampant increase in plastic and the resultant increase in waste are staggering. The earth cannot absorb the discarded plastic, which will remain for generations to come after our death. We are thus doing great harm to future generations.

In the past, forests were outside and temples were inside human hearts. Today, temples are outside and our heart has become a wilderness.

Everything is Divine

A few people, who prided themselves on being rationalists, came to meet Amma. Amma told them, "For Amma, everything in nature is God. In truth, there is nothing other than God. That is why our culture teaches us to respect and revere nature. People like you propagated the idea that such teachings are primitive. As a result, those who used to revere nature and who worshiped sacred groves lost faith in their beliefs and traditions and harmed nature. Now that people have come to realize the necessity of protecting the environment, millions are being spent on planting trees, digging ponds and protecting forests. There was no deforestation when nature was venerated. When a tree needed to be cut down, our elders would find a propitious date and time to do so. It was akin to fixing an auspicious day for marriage. They would perform a *pūjā* (ceremonial worship) and pray to the tree, "Please forgive us. We are cutting you down only because of a great need." Amma has heard Sugunacchan (her father) praying in this way. Trees would be cut down only if it was unavoidable. They would also plant tree saplings to compensate for the one they had felled. Protecting sacred groves and ponds were an integral part of life. It is this noble culture that rationalists, who prided themselves on their intellect, rejected as primitive. Now, the very same people are publicizing the need to protect the environment.

See the Big in the Small

Once, when Amma was a child, Damayanti-amma asked her to pluck five leaves from a jackfruit tree; these leaves were used as spoons to drink *kañji* (rice gruel). When Amma went to pluck the leaves, she saw a small, broken branch hanging by only a strip of bark. It had about 20 leaves on it. Amma took this twig to Damayanti-amma, who spanked her with the same twig. Finally, she said, "When you needed to take only five leaves, why did you break the whole twig?" What Damayanti-amma said was true. It is alright to take fallen leaves or those that are ripe and on the verge of falling. But when we break a twig, we are reducing its lifespan. Not only that, if those leaves had remained on the twig, they would have purified the air for a few more days. It was only after she had finished spanking Amma that Damayanti-amma learned that the twig was already broken. Nevertheless, Amma learned a valuable lesson. Even today, she feels pain in her heart if she sees anyone plucking a leaf needlessly.

In those days, while sweeping the courtyard, a few *īrkkili*[16] would fall away from the broom; or

---

[16] Bristles of a broom made from the midribs of leaves from a single coconut frond.

one or two might snap. Damayanti-amma would come over and say, "You're not holding the broom properly. Hold it with both hands while sweeping!" She would then show me how. If an īrkkili still fell out again, she would snatch the broom from me, spank me with it, and say, "Today, one īrkkili fell out. Tomorrow, another will, and in a few days, there will be no broom left!" Immediately, Amma would feel in her heart, "What Damayanti-amma is saying is true. The loss of one īrkkili after another will lead to the loss of the entire broom." Damayanti-amma thus taught Amma to see the whole broom in an īrkkili and not to see anything as small or insignificant. This is how she taught us *śraddhā*—complete focus on each action.

We were not allowed to talk while grinding the ingredients used to make curry, in case our spittle fell on what we were grinding. In those days, we used dry leaves and coconut husk to light the kitchen fire. Soot would stick to the sides of the pot and on the lid. Damayanti-amma would tell us, "Before opening the lid, blow on the sides of the pot to clear away the soot. Otherwise, when you open the lid, the soot will fall into the pot."

Damayanti-amma's instructions helped us remain attentive while doing anything.

Back then, paddy would be boiled, sun dried and winnowed to separate the grains from the husk. The dried and boiled grains would be pounded to get kernels. Usually, a few grains would scatter to the ground during the pounding. We would pick them up and put them back into the mortar. If Damayanti-amma saw the grains falling out, she would scold and sometimes even spank Amma. She would ask, "Can you create even one grain? Do you know how much effort goes into the creation of one grain? One paddy seed grows into a plant from which we can harvest many stalks of paddy rice. We must remember this when we see a single grain."

We get vegetables and fruits because of honey bees, which pollinate the plants. Honey bees fly two to three kilometers daily to collect nectar from flowers. In earlier days, the bees knew the way back to their hives even if they wandered afar. But now, scientists have found that they are losing their way and are unable to reach their hives. The main cause of their forgetfulness is the pesticides sprayed on plants and flowers. While sipping nectar from flowers sprayed with pesticides, the bees ingest poisonous chemicals that destroy their memory. Unable to return to their hives, many bees drop dead. If bees become extinct, many forms of plant life will disappear from earth and we will face starvation.

Amma almost never allows her ashram children to pluck freshly blossomed flowers. She has instructed them to gather only flowers that have fallen or are on the verge of falling. If we refrain from plucking fresh flowers, bees can gather nectar from them and make food for themselves, and the flowers will have a longer lifespan. This is why Amma prefers that devotees engage in worship through visualization. Of course, Amma will not tell people who earn their livelihood through flowers not to pluck them.

Nowadays, many people who collect honey from forests set fire to the beehives, killing all the bees. Only then do they collect the honey. They do not think about the harm they are doing to nature by killing the bees. Even forest dwellers of the past never did that. They would shoot arrows into the hive, and collect the honey dripping down in pots kept underneath. There are so many ways in which honey can be collected without killing bees. But because of the selfishness and cruelty in human hearts, people are not patient enough to collect honey in non-destructive ways.

Long ago, Amma used to go to neighboring houses to collect tapioca skin and water in which rice had been washed, to feed the cows. She would go in the evening to collect them. Once, when Amma went to one of the homes, she saw the children lying down, famished. Their mother explained, "I've not been able to feed the children today. Their father has gone fishing and has not returned. He will bring something when he comes back."

Amma asked, "Why don't you borrow some money to buy food for the children?"

The mother replied, "Yesterday, their father walked six kilometers to a relative's house to borrow some money, but the relative did not have any money. My husband has also not been able to catch any fish in the last two or three days."

That night, the father returned home very late. In the moonlight, he saw a turtle laying eggs on the seashore. After the turtle returned to the sea, the man collected half of the eggs, brought them home, and fed the children. The children asked, "Father, why didn't you take all the eggs?"

He replied, "If I'd taken all the eggs, the turtle would have been very sad. I have eight children. If I lose all of you, think of how grief-stricken I'll be. The turtle will also grieve like me. But if at least a few eggs hatch, it won't be so sad. When we had nothing to eat, we were sustained by the eggs of this turtle. If there are no turtles in the future, from where will we get eggs to eat when we're hungry?"

Even while suffering from the pangs of hunger, the father thought of the welfare of another being. Nowadays, people catch and export turtles that swim to the shore to lay eggs there. We are destroying future generations of turtles for the sake of money. This is how human beings are destroying everything in nature.

Long ago, people used to think about others even while they were suffering. Today, we will not hesitate to appease our hunger even if means causing sorrow to others. We must change this attitude. It will only lead to our downfall. Pushing another species to the brink of extinction by our deeds is akin to plunging a knife into our own body. We are not separate from nature. Our ancestors realized this, and taught us to worship all beings in nature, including plants, trees, animals and birds. This reverence for creatures big and small is not a show but an expression of gratitude to nature for all the help she renders. The modes of worship of our ancestors were not primitive. On the contrary, it is we, who have no gratitude to nature and who are bent on harming her, who are primitive. If we revered nature, we would protect her.

The Fullness of Gratitude

There is no use in merely bemoaning the atrocities we are inflicting on nature. In order to prevent further harm, we must be ready to change many of our present habits and current lifestyle. We must follow the traditions of our ancestors, with the proper understanding. Once we become aware of the interdependence of ecosystems and of the extraordinary service that nature is providing us, we will be ready to love, revere and worship everything in nature. Every one of our actions will reflect the fullness of gratitude towards nature.

May humankind gain this wisdom and goodness of heart. May the Almighty bless my children.

Pronunciation Guide

Vowels can be short or long:
a – as 'u' in but; ā – as 'a' in far
e – as 'a' in may; ē – as 'a' in name
i – as 'i' in pin; ī – as 'ee' in meet
o – as in oh; ō – as 'o' in mole
u – as 'u' in push; ū – as 'oo' in hoot

ṛ – as ri in crisp
ḥ – pronounce 'aḥ' like 'aha,' 'iḥ' like 'ihi,' and 'uḥ' like 'uhu.'

Some consonants are aspirated (e.g. kh); others are not (e.g. k). The examples given below are only approximate:
k – as 'k' in 'kite;' kh – as 'ckh' in 'Eckhart'
g – as 'g' in 'give;' gh – as 'g-h' in 'dig-hard'
c – as 'c' in 'cello;' ch – as 'ch-h' in 'staunch-heart'
j – as 'j' in 'joy;' jh – as 'dgeh' in 'hedgehog'
p – as 'p' in 'pine;' ph – as 'ph' in 'up-hill'
b – as 'b' in 'bird;' bh – as 'bh' in 'rub-hard'

r – as 'r' in ride
ñ – as 'ny' in 'canyon;' ṅ – as 'ng' in 'sing'

The letters ḍ, ṭ, ṇ are pronounced with the tip of the tongue against the hard palate, the others with the tip against the teeth.

ṭ – as 't' in 'tub;' ṭh – as 'th' in 'lighthouse'
ḍ – as 'd' in 'dove;' ḍh – as 'dh' in 'red-hot'
ṇ – as 'n' in 'naught'
ḷ – as 'l' in 'revelry'
ṣ – as 'sh' in 'shine;' ś – as 's' in German 'sprechen'

With double consonants the sound is pronounced twice:
cc – as 'tc' in 'hot chip'
jj – as 'dj' in 'red jet'

www.ingramcontent.com/pod-product-compliance
Lightning Source LLC
Chambersburg PA
CBHW070635050426
42450CB00011B/3210
* 9 7 8 1 6 8 0 3 7 8 8 7 0 *